11/15

D1200723

MONSTROUS MANNERS

MANNERS AT A FRIEND'S HOUSE

BY BRIDGET HEOS

ILLUSTRATED BY KATYA LONGHI

Amicus Illustrated is published by Amicus
P.O. Box 1329, Mankato, MN 56002
www.amicuspublishing.us

Library of Congress Cataloging-in-Publication Data
Heos, Bridget, author.
Manners at a friend's house / by Bridget Heos ;
Illustrated by Katya Longhi.
pages cm. — (Monstrous manners)
Summary: "A young monster with no manners
visits his friend's house and learns the manners he
should use while visiting"— Provided by publisher.
ISBN 978-1-60753-743-4 (library binding)
ISBN 978-1-60753-843-1 (ebook)
1. Etiquette for children and teenagers—Juvenile
literature. I. Longhi, Katya, illustrator. II. Title.
BJ1857.C5H46 2016
395.1'22—dc23 2014036512

Editor: Rebecca Glaser
Designer: Kathleen Petelinsek

Printed in the United States of America at
Corporate Graphics in North Mankato, Minnesota.

10 9 8 7 6 5 4 3 2 1

ABOUT THE AUTHOR

Bridget Heos is the author of more than 70 books for children, including *Mustache Baby* and *Mustache Baby Meets His Match*. Her favorite manners are holding the door for others and jumping up to help. You can find out more about her, if you please, at *www.authorbridgetheos.com*.

ABOUT THE ILLUSTRATOR

Katya Longhi was born in southern Italy. She studied illustration at the Nemo NT Academy of Digital Arts in Florence. She loves to create dream worlds with horses, flying dogs, and princesses in her illustrations. She currently lives in northern Italy with her Prince Charming.

Stop jumping on our couch, Monster! Our mom will send you home for having bad manners. I know you want to stay and play. How about if we teach you good manners?

Let's start over outside.

What do you do when you come to the door?

No, no, Monster. You don't bust down the door. You must ring the doorbell.

One time is enough, Monster.

No, Monster. Be polite. Say hello first.

Wow! That was really nice, Monster.

This isn't a restaurant, Monster. Don't ask for food, even if you ask nicely. You can eat when the rest of the family eats.

"Hi, Ricardo! Hey, what's this?"
"That's my mom's!"
You need to play with toys, not breakable stuff, Monster!

"Ricardo, do you have any ninja toys?"
"They're in the closet."
Don't make a mess. Just get out the toys you want.

If you do make a mess, at least
clean it up when you're done playing.

"Hey, you want to play soccer?"
"Not really, Ricardo."

Try again, Monster. It's polite to do things your friend wants to do. You can choose next.

When playing a game, be a good sport. Follow the rules. If you win, don't brag. If you lose, don't pout.

Monster, now it's your turn
to choose a game to play.

Not so fast! Wash your hands,
and then sit down at the table.

And don't grab! Wait for the food to be passed and for rest of the family to start eating. They may want to say prayers first.

If you don't like what's for dinner, keep it to yourself. Take a few bites. Think of something nice to say. The cook worked hard on this meal.

Look, your dad is here to pick you up.
How do you leave a friend's house politely?

Don't run off and hide, Monster. When it's time to go, say goodbye. And don't forget to say thank you!

Hey, you're not a monster after all. You're our neighbor Jackson. Good job learning manners. Now, our mom will let you come over again!

GOOD MANNERS WHEN VISITING FRIENDS

1. Knock and wait to be invited in.
2. Be polite and take time to say hello to all family members.
3. Don't ask for food. Wait for snack or meal time.
4. Don't touch breakable things.
5. If you make a mess, clean it up right away.
6. Follow the rules of games. Don't gloat or pout.
7. Take turns playing what you and your friend want to play.
8. Wait for the rest of the family before eating dinner.
9. Say only nice things about the food.
10. When it's time to leave, say thank you and leave right away.

READ MORE

Burstein, John. *Manners Please! Why it Pays to Be Polite*. New York: Crabtree, 2011.

Ingalls, Ann. *Being a Good Guest*. Mankato, Minn.: The Child's World, 2013.

Keller, Laurie. *Do Unto Otters: a Book About Manners*. New York: Henry Holt, 2007.

Tourville, Amanda Doering. *Manners at a Friend's House*. Minneapolis: Picture Window Books, 2009.

WEBSITES

Can You Teach My Alligator Manners?
disneyjunior.com/can-you-teach-my-alligator-manners
Watch videos and do activities to learn about manners in all different places, including restaurants, school, and more.

Learn about Manners: Crafts and Activities for Kids
www.dltk-kids.com/crafts/miscellaneous/manners.htm
Try these songs, crafts, and coloring pages to learn and practice good manners.

Top Table Manners for Kids
www.emilypost.com/home-and-family-life/children-and-teens/408-top-table-manners-for-kids
Learn more about table manners from expert Emily Post.